feeling sick?

Sore Throat

By Jillian Powell

Contents

WHAT'S WRONG?

When you have a sore throat,
it is hard to swallow. Your throat
feels dry and tickly or scratchy.
It may look red inside.
Sometimes your **tonsils** and
the **glands** in your neck are
swollen too. You may start to
feel unwell.

6

Dear Doc

What can I do for a
sore throat?

Try gargling *with a
little salt mixed with
some warm water.*

Did you know?

Sucking throat drops helps you make more saliva so it is easier to swallow.

7

WHAT CAUSES SORE THROATS?

Most sore throats are caused by **viruses**. They are spread by coughing or sneezing or by touch. Some can make you lose your voice for a while.

If you start shivering and sneezing, you probably have a cold coming. You can also get a sore throat from a virus such as chickenpox or measles.

8

Dear Doc

I am losing my voice. What can I do?

The best thing is to rest your voice and drink plenty of water.

Noah's story

I woke up with a sore throat and my voice sounded funny. A cold started the next day and I began to shiver and sneeze!

WHAT'S GOING ON?

When **germs** get into your body, they start to multiply. Your body makes **mucus** in your nose and throat to try to flush them out. Your body also starts to make **antibodies** to fight the virus. Your throat may get irritated and become sore and tickly.

Did you know?

Breathing through your mouth because of a blocked nose can make your throat feel sore.

10

Dear Doc

Why do I cough when I have a cold?

Your body makes you cough to try to clear mucus from your throat and lungs.

11

STREP THROAT

Some sore throats are caused by germs called **bacteria**. The most common bacteria is streptococcus (strep). It can make your throat red and sore. You may have yellow or white spots on your tongue and tonsils. You may also have a **fever** and a headache. Doctors can give you **antibiotics** to make you better.

12

Dear Doc

How do I know if I have strep throat?

The doctor can do a swab *test for the strep throat germ.*

I had to have a test to see if I had strep throat. The doctor asked me to open my mouth wide. He took a swab but it didn't hurt at all.

Dear Doc

Why does my throat get sore after I've been cheering at soccer?

Shouting and cheering can strain the muscles in your throat.

14

SORE THROATS AND ALLERGIES

Sore throats can be caused by allergies. An allergy to pollen, animals, or **pollution** can make your throat sore. You can also get a sore throat from dry air, or from talking or shouting a lot. Smoking causes sore throats and other serious throat diseases.

Did you know?

Central heating makes the air dry and can cause sore throats. *Humidifiers* sometimes help.

TONSILLITIS

Some throat germs can cause tonsillitis. This is when your tonsils swell up and become red and sore. Sometimes they look white or yellow too. Your neck glands may swell up and you may have a fever and a headache.

16

Did you know?

Tonsils trap germs in your throat and make antibodies to fight them.

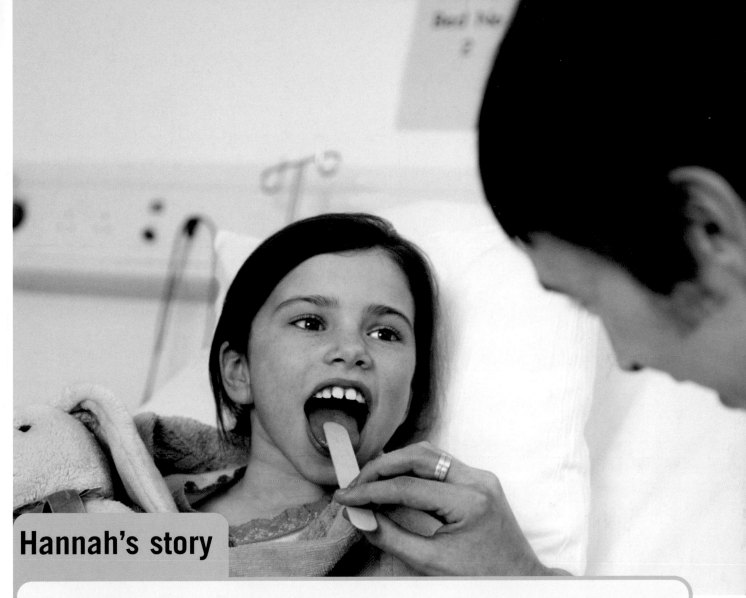

Hannah's story

I had to go to the hospital to have my tonsils out because I kept getting tonsillitis. The doctors and nurses were really kind there.

Rena's story

When I had a sore throat, the doctor told me that my body would get better faster if I had plenty of sleep and rest.

GETTING BETTER

When you have a sore throat, you may not feel hungry. Foods like soup and jello are easy to swallow when your throat hurts. Drink lots of water as it will help your body flush out the germs.

Did you know?

A spoonful of honey can help to soothe a sore throat.

STAYING HEALTHY

You can help your body fight off the germs that cause sore throats. Eat healthy foods such as fresh fruit and vegetables, which are full of **vitamin C**. Plenty of exercise will also help your body make antibodies to boost your **immune system**.

20

Did you know?

We catch more germs in winter because they spread more easily when people are indoors together.

Dear Doc

How can I help keep my throat healthy?

Drink plenty of water every day.

Glossary

Antibiotics   drugs that can help your body fight some germs

Antibodies   chemicals made in your blood by white blood cells to fight germs

Bacteria   germs that cause food poisoning and other illnesses

Fever   when the body's temperature is higher than it normally is (98.6°F/37°C)

Germs   a tiny living thing that can cause illness

Gargle   when you blow air through liquid in your throat without swallowing it

Glands   groups of cells that do a particular job in the body

Humidifiers   something that works to put moisture into the air

Immune system   the way your body defends itself against germs and diseases

Mucus   sticky stuff made by cells in the nose and throat

Pollution   dirt in the air or ground from factories and cars

Swab   using a cotton pad to take a small sample of body fluids

Swollen   larger than normal

Tonsils   glands either side of the throat that fight germs

Viruses   germs that cause colds and other illnesses

Vitamin C   a substance found in foods including fruit and vegetables that we need to stay healthy and fight illnesses